Messy
on the Inside

Eileen Albrizio

ACKNOWLEDGEMENTS

TRAPPED UNDER THE WEIGHT OF THE AUTUMN HALF-MOON,
Underwood Review, Summer 1998
AUGUST, *Natural Networker*, Jun-Jul 1998

First Edition.

MESSY ON THE INSIDE

ISBN: 1-889289-32-9

Library of Congress Catalog Card Number: 98-90744

Printed in the USA by Morris Publishing
                    3212 E. Hwy 30
                    Kearney, NE 68847

for
Wayne
I love you
always

unfailing appreciation to
Connie & Fran

special thanks to
Victoria
Artemis Rising

INTRODUCTION

To enter the landscape depicted in Eileen Albrizio's poetry is to venture into a world of inverted fecundity, an exquisitely literate marshland teeming with loss, longing, grief and despair yet blooming with startling images of unity made only more precious by their poverty.

With exacting diction, Eileen relentlessly unveils the harsher realities of abuse, neglect, isolation, illness and death. From "I watched you crack the stubborn shells/of cherrystones, raw and plump and pink" and "[the odor is...] caramelized sugar engulfed in decay,/tepid, hanging motionless in the air" to "Just space,/ where hollow replaces heart/and echo replaces beat" and "Rain's shriving/laughter rattles the roof," this ambitious first collection firmly takes root.

Eileen's passion for structure imbues her poems' sometimes astonishingly dark world with a consoling, incantatory quality. She deftly adopts and preserves well- and lesser-known poetic forms including sestina, sonnet, terza rima, haiku and kyrielle, to name a few. I consider her choice of a villanelle for "A Child's Fall." Using powerfully understated language, the poem's speaker, now grown, recalls the anguish of losing a brother and a parent's careless censure of her grief. Yet it is through the chosen form — with its rhythmic repetition and intricate, swaying rhyme scheme — that the speaker's timeless burden of repressed grief and guilt and pain is made most palpable.

And then, almost without warning, we are given "A little patch of green extends her universe/....She can sense the living world." Later, "All day and night a chorus sings/in perfect half-billion part harmony." And finally, most redemptive of all, after witnessing — at least for a fleeting instant — her undeniable connection to an entirely exquisite universe, one speaker's conclusion that "So lies my significance."

As a sister poet in the writer's circle *Artemis Rising* and coach of the 1998 Connecticut National Slam Poetry Team, I am most fortunate to work with Eileen and to benefit from her talent, determination and meticulous attention to detail. As an early reader of this promising collection, I am moved by her unflinching candor, fluidity, and yes, grace.

K. Ann Cavanaugh
New Haven, 21 July 1998

Table of Contents

GROWING

Poverty and proliferation go hand in hand,
as was the case when my cells split some decades ago.
The youngest of many I watched the older ones grow
bored and unattended. Nothing gained and nothing planned.

In a childhood dream I received a doll as a gift.
I held her tight within my grip so she'd still be there
when I awoke. I hoped to find a doll with long hair
and adjustable parts, whose elbows bend and legs lift.

When I opened my eyes and unclenched my fist, I found
no doll, just the imprints my nails made upon my palm.
I was surprised and disappointed that in the calm
of sleep I was unable to keep what I had bound.

The next night I dreamt of a candy bar. I held fast.
But I awoke to no melted chocolate on the sheet,
and following nights, despite my attempts to repeat
the test, I found the substance of my dreams didn't last.

Once I longed for toys and sweets, things I could not possess.
Now the world lay at my feet. I look about my room.
Intangible treasures welcome me into this womb
I have created. Although I have more, I opt for less.

In my opulence I have no children of my own.
My older siblings are still bored and unattended.
And I still bear the mark of what I once pretended,
in my dreams, in my hand, yet I know that I have grown.

THE THINNING OF FILOMENA
a rimas dissolutas

Steam from the egg-drop soup kissed my lips
as I watched you crack the stubborn shells
of cherrystones, raw and plump and pink.
Tomato shrimp simmered to a boil.

Layers of china, mismatched with chips,
dressed the table. Lemon-seafood smells
poked at my nose. I stood by the sink
avoiding the hot, spattering oil

that crisped the battered squid. I stole sips
of wine, distorting the rhythmic swells
of clanking pots, splashing water, clink
of glasses. You added to the soil

on your apron as you swiped your hips
with floured hands. Distant Sunday bells
announced it was time to eat. To think
of the feasts, remembering you toil

preparing those sumptuous banquets strips
the lines from your hollow cheeks, and quells
the hunger for days when food and drink
were joyful for you. Now you recoil

at nourishment, and the IV drips
sustenance into your veins. Your spells
of suicidal hysterics shrink
with medication. Your stockings coil

at your thin ankles. Every bone rips
through the skin at your joints. The nurse yells
for you to eat. Your eyes barely blink,
and the shrimp, like the memories, spoil.

A CHILD'S FALL

a villanelle

I remember falling to my knees,
pulled by your hand to pray around the bed.
You wept for him. I didn't say a word.

He was the son impossible to please,
though your efforts were immense, still he fled.
I remember falling to my knees,

throwing a tantrum that you never heard.
Burdened by my life you wished me dead.
You wept for him. I didn't say a word.

As a daughter I never could appease
your anguish over losing him, instead
I remember falling to my knees,

weak from the loss of blood, my vision blurred.
What a selfish little girl, you said.
You wept for him. I didn't say a word.

Inflamed by my affection and my pleas,
you snapped and slapped my face and shook your head.
I remember falling to my knees.
You wept for him. I didn't say a word.

YOU TAUGHT ME WELL

I was taught very young I had to live by
the tenets of a segregated church,
where men stood at pulpits, hands raised to the sky,
and the congregation looked up in search
of the god speaking through the figurehead
I was told to revere without query.
I drank the blood of a martyr long dead.
Feared my own thoughts, for I was taught very
young that thoughts alone could send me to hell.
That god punished those who masturbated.
Every sin I was required to tell
to the priest my brother told me he hated;
the priest who fondled him under his robe
when he stood on the altar as a boy.
My mother said we're to suffer like Job,
should expect to live a life without joy.
I was taught very young that homely girls
became nuns who serviced the needs of men,
and smiled in the faces of churls,
then abandoned hope of smiling again.
Homosexuals were execrated.
Poets considered the devil's escort.
And mother, you said we were created
from the ribs of Adam to be his consort.
You played the perfect subservient role,
bearing on decree my unwanted life.
The belief that god planted the seed stole
your love for your child, your love as a wife.
You branded my sex when I came of age.
Burned e.e. cummings found under the bed.
Beat down my passion for music and stage.
Banned Ibsen, Strindberg, O'Neil. Instead
I studied the word of a vengeful god.
Knew I'd been stained by the most heinous sin,
and begged to be cleansed as I knelt to laud
the one whom you said would heal me in
the name of the father, son and holy ghost.
Pitiable, wretched, dirty I prayed
to recover a soul lost amidst a host

of others, like me, who had disobeyed.
We're born into a world without choice.
Blind in a faith meant to keep us in place.
Stripped of artistry, progress and voice.
Preaching hypocrisy. Lacking in grace.
Once, considered less than an afterthought,
I witnessed the death of what I held dear,
in me and you. Very young I was taught
to hate the god I was told to revere.

EQUIVOCATION

You're fairly important to me, he said.
The phrase hit my ears and ran through my head,
then bounced off my heart, held grip on my breath,
and gave me the strength to overcome death.

It took me a day to know what he meant.
Carefully picked were the words that he sent.
Fairly, not *very.* Moderate at best.
Tertiary. Placed behind all the rest.

You're a supplement to my life, he said.
Immediately I was filled with dread.
I could not delight in the compliment
to decorate him like an ornament.
I don't care to be an accessory,
like video games, or cable TV.

He's never called me beautiful, but he
has said he's somewhat attracted to me.

You're new job's a good steppingstone, he said.
Now I'm certain that I had not misread
that my achievements just weren't good enough.
All that I'd done was considered mere fluff.

My desire to explicate every word
left fragmented remarks often absurd.
Would I be happy if I were to find
the text incisive, untethered and kind?

You're different from everyone else, he said.
It hit with such force I wished I were dead.
To say that I'm different is very abstract.
I had no idea how I should react.

Each statement defined is up for debate,
as long as he needs to prevaricate.
Am I deliberately being mislead?
You're a very sensitive girl, he said.

TRAPPED UNDER THE WEIGHT OF THE AUTUMN HALF-MOON

Quarter past two. The metronome beats. A herald
for grief. My companion, the distorted shadow
of the sycamore branch, is forced across my ribs
by the autumn half-moon. I contemplate the fibs
told by myriad lovers who secretly know
where I lie tonight, pining for their sex. Periled.

Warm for this time of year. Tears symbiont with sweat.
My hands dirty, glide across my breast, guided by
a pernicious ghost companion, the distorted
shadow of the sycamore branch. All aborted
lusts resurge in the moment of entry as I
convulse in this canopy bed, grievous and wet.

Aroused and reeling from the spin of blood, I grope
for the shadow of my lover, the sycamore
branch. But the distorted companion fades as clouds
pass over the autumn half-moon. The darkness shrouds
this empty room. I think of one I knew before
to push my hollow passion and secluded hope.

Despondent waves flood my lungs, force climactic gasps.
Throat raw from each burst of breath, I yell to no one.
The sound hits the ceiling, bounces off the lonely
walls. Echoes, wanes, then disappears, for the only
one near is deaf. It can not hear, my companion.
Distorted shadow of the sycamore branch clasps

its arms around my waist. I'm rendered motionless
by the weight of the autumn half-moon. With the scratch
of the sycamore branch on my window, I mourn
what I have become, one my companion would scorn
if it could speak. It escapes before I can catch
this distorted shadow. I wait for its caress.

ABOVE WORDS

Wasted is the spoken word
unless that word is received.
At least this is what I've heard.
    Ever fearful to speak it,
    should the listener be deceived,
    perchance to misinterpret.
Known to be an equivoque,
what is, or is not believed,
can't fault to the one who spoke.
    If another has defined,
    then the speaker has been thieved,
    ultimately undermined.
So, best leave the word unsaid,
in case it should be retrieved
by one muddled in the head.
    The dangers vary, I know,
    for many times I have grieved
    over words that tend to grow
beyond my comprehension,
esoteric, yet perceived
engulfed in apprehension.
    For example, the term *love*
    has at one time pleased and peeved,
    synchronously, not above
meaning *hate* or *lust* or *pain.*
The most abstruse, most bereaved
of every word, most arcane.
    More than enunciation,
    vowels and consonants heaved
    to create intonation,
but inflection of the brow,
or the way the breaths relieved.
Gritted teeth, clenched fists allow
    the auricular translation
    to be judged as was conceived.
    Unless...abstract oration
makes the phrase a bit obscure.
Axioms to which I've cleaved
blend together in a blur,

      enveloped in deception,
      bound with hunches, lies and sheaved
      with careless misconception.
No hope of being freed,
temporarily reprieved
from confines of text. What's more,
      once planted in the ear,
      germinated, bloomed and leaved,
      makes it difficult to hear.
Oh, dependent on the word.
The prison where it's received
makes me wish it never heard.

THE SECRET

a pantoum

Starting as a furtive game played in the darkness,
I felt your breath but I couldn't see your features.
You sighed hot against my ear, *This won't hurt a bit,*
then laid the palm of your hand against my face.

I felt your breath but I couldn't see your features
as you turned to mist beginning at your feet,
then laid the palm of your hand against my face
just before the transmutation was complete.

As you turned to mist beginning at your feet,
dampness penetrated my skin. I felt you,
just before the transmutation was complete,
in my blood. From the world you were out of view.

Dampness penetrated my skin. I felt you
while you journeyed along the path of regrets
in my blood. From the world you were out of view.
You settled in among the sins and secrets.

While you journeyed along the path of regrets,
I prepared your home in the back of my brain.
You settled in among the sins and secrets.
Without pause began your quest to cause me pain.

I prepared your home in the back of my brain.
You sighed hot against my ear, *This won't hurt a bit.*
Without pause began your quest to cause me pain.
All from a furtive game played in the darkness.

OLD WOUNDS
a villanelle

The doctor said there shouldn't be a scar.
In time I would forget the whole ordeal.
I'm waiting for the marks to disappear.

He said the tiny stitches wouldn't mar
my skin. But the cicatrix I could feel.
The doctor said there shouldn't be a scar.

There were rules to which I had to adhere
in order for the wounds to neatly seal.
I'm waiting for the marks to disappear.

A difficult convalescence by far.
I was warned the scabs I mustn't peel.
The doctor said there shouldn't be a scar.

I wear the memory after a year,
a reminder that my attempts were real.
I'm waiting for the marks to disappear.

I'm readily aware of where they are,
these blemishes I try hard to conceal.
The doctor said there shouldn't be a scar.
I'm waiting for the marks to disappear.

I LOVE YOU TO DEATH

I love you to death.
The last time I saw her she hugged me and told me that.
They removed a lot of her. Enough of her remained.
Short regrowth about her ears opened my eyes to hers.
Hair once long, dark, thick, styled, and always framing her face,
seemed shorter to those who hadn't seen her in a while.
But those of us who knew joked about how it's better
than peach fuzz she covered with a scarf two months ago.

I love you to death.
Her eyes spoke the words just before the truth stung my ears.
She giggled. Funny the autonomy death possessed.
The endless depth of her eyes harbored pain, sparkled hope.
She wrapped her arms around me on that chilled autumn day.
Her life soaked through my coat, warm and more real than my own.
She boarded the train for home six hundred miles away.
Smiled and softly said *I'll see you soon.* Sealed her fate with

I love you to death.
The train grew smaller. A movie rolled behind my eyes.
New Year's Eve, before our toast, we kissed her head for luck,
bald, except for a few random strands, then raised a glass,
made our silent sacrifices. Prayed for her to live.
Convinced ourselves someone heard, but didn't dare wonder
where we'd be at this time next year. The train disappeared.
Its whistle blew in tune with the words she sang to me.

I love you to death.

BROKEN

Not long ago his smile raced through the door
before his feet even crossed the threshold.
At twelve, endless tales of adventure spilled
from innocent lips. Stories that would soar
on independent wings swooped down, took hold
of my heart. Together we would fly, thrilled

by the weightlessness of his youth, above
the clouds. Up there the world was his to own.
An ingenuous journey, guided by
a nod, a wink, a wish, a wren, a dove.
Our destinations were always unknown
and we could only get there from the sky.

Not long ago his smile raced through the door
before his feet even crossed the threshold.
Something about school, his teacher, the day
tumbled off his excited tongue. Folklore
of a twelve-year-old boy. Tales that unfold
reveal an untainted child at play.

Schoolboy abandon, taken for granted.
Constant. Bright with the sun. Brushed with the breeze.
Close with his friends and adults he could trust.
Always in motion, yet firmly planted
in family, in custom, at home. With ease
he was taken in by the world, and just

as he was taking it in, the sun stopped
shining. The air was still. The day silent,
and dark. Very dark. He doesn't fly now.
The world he created in the sky dropped
from the clouds, hit the ground with a violent
crash. Destroyed. And as I remember how

not long ago his smile raced through the door
before his feet even crossed the threshold,
I hear the now familiar sound of legs
against sheets. He doesn't smile anymore.
Says he's too sick for school. Sick with a cold
again. And in the night he cries and begs

for someone, or something to stop. *Please stop.*
I wake him, to calm him, to wipe away
the residue of his nightmare, his tears.
He shifts. Rustle. Legs against sheets. His mop
of hair matted with sweat. He won't betray
the dark angels of his dreams, of his fears.

He closes his eyes, feigning sleep, I know
from the sporadic, shallow spurts of breath
that turn into sobs later in the night.
He won't speak, but every day his eyes show
to reveal his secret would cause the death
of more than his innocence. That it might

kill him. Might kill me. He can't hold my hand,
cowering from the scrape of flesh on flesh.
A trembling starts when I say I've spoken
to his teacher asking for insight, and
the tremble grows so great it creates fresh
wounds, and the boy, still twelve, has been broken.

Crouched with hands wrapped around his knees, seems more
like small prey than a child. Though it's not cold
he shivers. I remember the day when,
not long ago, his smile raced through the door
before his feet even crossed the threshold,
and know that will never happen again.

THE WAR AGAINST IMMUNODEFICIENCY

They crept inside you while you were coming of age,
these surreptitious killers, skulking through your blood,
building a silent army, preparing to flood
your thymus and spleen. They would carry out their rage

in a surprise attack upon the white forces
that were supposed to protect you from invasion.
You became defenseless against the pervasion
of assassins, incognizant of the courses

they took to carry out the stratagem that broke
you down, bit by bit. After a decade of war,
crouched in the trenches, weary and wounded, you swore
you'd win or die trying. Unable to provoke

a truce, your lungs were assaulted, and then your brain.
The enemy set up camp on your memory.
You forgot your own name. You could no longer see.
Their position was such they could drive you insane.

When reports came in from the front about your capture,
we knew you were unarmed, alone, unprotected.
All attempts at reinforcements were rejected.
The assailants knew they could crack you through torture.

Before they had a chance to move in, you let go.
At first we thought they'd won. Although their numbers grew,
their lives were linear. But in life and death, you
have become legend and icon. Today you show

us yesterday. Tomorrow we walk side by side.
Walls of intolerance were destroyed in the war,
and now free to cross the borders, we can explore
a new world, and embrace what you fought for with pride.

JEFF

The laughter began with Whoopie Goldberg,
lingered in the lobby of the movie
theatre, then ripped through us like an iceberg
through Alaskan water. Our revelry

did not set out to make a scene, but you,
famous for funny in our little world,
held the antic tight in your stomach. Grew
bloated until the hilarity hurled

from your mouth, ricocheted off the popcorn
display, soda machine, and suddenly
comical standup of Sly Stallone. Born
from kernels, cola, licorice candy,

and deceptive black of the midday night
that enveloped the fantasy seekers
once swinging doors swooshed shut, tenebrous light
gave way to previews, surround sound speakers

exploded life, and you and I, each friend
to the other and the characters on
the screen, pointed and whispered till the end.
That was then. A moment of abandon.

A boisterous bubble destined to burst.
I knew you were sick. You told me, then shrugged
and fired fatal sarcasm at the worst
yet to come. I only wish I had hugged

you the day words of dying hung, alive
yet quiet in the room. Thickened like brume,
creating a fog that would someday drive
us apart. I could no longer assume

you would exist forever. You began
organizing finances and planning
gatherings to bring our long-estranged clan
together. I stood on the side, fanning

the flame of denial. You weren't here yet
thirty years. Younger than me. Determined
to defy fate though you'd erased regret
because no one had ever undermined

Death. In the instant a lifetime became
defined, your arms spread wider to embrace
a world that, for you, would not be the same.
When your skeleton appeared on your face,

sunken cheeks and eyes, pants hung low on hips,
a watch too bulky for your wrist, you smiled
through ever-cracked and sometimes bleeding lips,
of which I deftly avoided. Your mild

complexion turned sallow. My large but hollow
eyes saw only what you wished me to see.
I loved you from where I could not follow,
for you were walking toward a place where sea

and sky and time and space and here and there
are everything, and everything was more
than this healthy, eternal soul could bare.
You were brother to me. That was before

your dying. Before, when you joked how you
would live at least one year longer than me
because I was one year older than you,
and wisecracked how you'd talk trash about me

when I'm gone. With a decade to prepare
you came to understand your destiny.
I refused to comprehend, would not share
you with Death. I thought a lot about me.

What would I do without you? Now I know.
Have become familiar with the crushing
blow to the soft part of my throat. The slow
motion return of the phone. The rushing

blood to my face as I realize I can't
call you with an anecdotal tidbit
about my day and dreams, and rave and rant
about little things anymore. Or sit

in pitch black movie theatre, each critic
of the highest order, discerning flaws
and perfection in every scene. The sick
entered you while you were young, without cause

killed you, left me to face my growing old.
I wish I had hugged you the day laughter
ripped through us like an iceberg. I want to hold
the time we stood in the lobby after

the movie, blissfully naïve, you, me,
Whoopie Goldberg and Sly Stallone. Best friends.
At night I dream the popcorn memory
and in my sleep the movie never ends.

A GLIMPSE

a pantoum

I see you're a bit messy on the inside
the way the blinds hang crooked in your window.
Through every aperture escapes a bright white light,
but for the cinderblock-sized openings below.

The way the blinds hang crooked in your window
allows a glimpse of a long pale southern wall.
But for the cinderblock-sized openings below
I catch a lot of you. The way the shadows fall

allows a glimpse of a long pale southern wall.
A lonely frame hangs not quite in the center.
I catch a lot of you. The way the shadows fall
is inviting, but I'm still afraid to enter.

A lonely frame hangs not quite in the center.
The subject dark with no details from where I stand
is inviting, but I'm still afraid to enter.
The suggestion of a chair, books, movement and

the subject dark with no details from where I stand.
I see you're a bit messy on the inside.
The suggestion of a chair, books, movement and
through every aperture escapes a bright white light.

THE CRITIC
an English Sonnet

Aloof, you sat down front to watch the show
and wore with pride your most pedantic face.
With hand to mouth you nodded in the know,
and intermittently displayed a trace
of disapproval. Knowing I could view
your every move, you shifted in your seat.
You hesitated when the piece was through.
In what appeared a patronizing beat,
you tossed my way a smatter of applause.
I left the stage, your head was turned away,
Then tapped your chin, reviewing all the flaws
that you have found within my pithy play.
You scurried out the door amidst the herd.
A clear critique without saying a word.

ANTIPATHY

a terza rima

Revulsive waves of force fall over you.
Before my eyes they hurl your body back
the very moment you and I are through.

The sparkle in your pupils turns to black,
and with a violent shiver shove me off.
You do not know that I can see the crack

in your veneer once ardent. When you scoff
about the consternation on my face,
I stammer a few words of love. You cough

to cover up the tender pleas, then race
away from me to make an urgent call.
If only you would choose to use some grace

in dealing with the harsh instinctive fall
of passion that occurs when someone eats
too much of something he desires. I stall.

I hope in vain the sight of me deletes
aversion that you feel. Instead I sprout
a vine around my heart. Entwined, it beats

a frenzied drum that proves beyond a doubt
it was the act that brought you here to me
and not the me that this was all about.

I hate myself in knowing I could be
the single source of your antipathy.

ISOLATION

a sestina

A little patch of green extends her universe
beyond the front door. She can sense the living world.
There are no fences, no walls or hedge barriers
to protect her from the elements, the dangers
of coexistence. The illusion of safety
surrounds her as long as she remains on the patch.
       To venture past the bastion that guards the patch,
       set foot on the pavement outside her universe,
       would bring certain, sudden, violent death. No safety
       for the wanderer. Hurt before, the shut-in's world
       becomes small, secluded and lonely, with no dangers.
       Eternal life in her citadel. Barriers
becoming thicker throughout the years. Barriers
made from the abstractions of fear. Outside the patch
cutthroats hide, carrying sacks containing dangers
of every design found in the universe.
She sits on her front stoop, and peers into a world
beyond invisible walls, the realms of safety,
       and wonders what it would be like to sport safety
       like a coat, and readily cross the barriers
       shielded from killers, thieves and rapists of the world.
       Veiled, obscure, no one would see her step off the patch,
       or hear her footsteps. Unseen in their universe,
       she could romp about the town sidestepping dangers.
Instead, she paces, hungry, counting the dangers
that lay in waiting past the confines of safety.
Five were slain and disemboweled in their universe.
Ten broke their necks failing to climb the barriers.
Hundreds hit by cars when they journeyed off the patch,
their heads crushed under the wheels of trucks. It's a world
       filled with near-misses and direct-hits. It's a world,
       she knows, diseased, contaminated with dangers
       outweighing benefits. Now and then her green patch
       is sprinkled by disparaging words that safety
       can't umbrella. The noon sun on the barriers
       casts shadows of aspersions. While their universe
breeds assassins, her remote world harbors safety.
She waves to the dangers that pass the barriers.
Ignored on her patch. Alone in her universe.

SERVING A PURPOSE
a rimas dissolutas

Clean, black apron. Worn rubber soles.
Button-down collar, sleeves, below
uniform vest. Sweated forehead.
Metallic kitchen wet from heat.
The smell of old food on my skin.

Half-filled glasses, barely touched bowls
of the most perfect gazpacho
before perfect patrons, who said
they loved the soup, but couldn't eat
any more. I clear their plates, grin

with appeasement, bring them more rolls
and another glass of wine. Slow
nights are the hardest. Hours ahead,
expecting few tips, and my feet
already hurt. One thought within,

like unseen patches over holes
in these old pants, *Someday, I know,*
I won't do this anymore. Dread
soothed as I pull hard for the sweet
tobacco, that only burns in

back of my throat, lingers and holes
up in my lungs. Sure death, I know,
but everybody here smokes. Thread-
bare existence, like my pants. Neat
tailored suits, get up, drop a fin

on the table. I watch. Their souls
free to leave. I'd leave, but I'm so
scared. They're smart, brave. I have no head
for the world, no power to cheat
fate. Wouldn't know where to begin.

Too small to handle the controls
of life. Strange how not long ago
I was young. Strange how life has led
me nowhere. Strange how my dreams beat
me down, where once I reveled in

their hope. I work. Creating goals
will surely bring defeat and show
the worst of me. I smoke instead
of eat. I smoke a lot. They seat
one more. My body weak, too thin

to carry heavy trays. The roles
they take on taunt me. I grow
tired, and cry a lot. Their lives fed
me. Now I see what I'm not. Seat
one more, and order up his gin.

BAD SEED

She was angry while you grew in her womb.
You were her third, and she knew, not her last.
Conceived in the first month of fifty-six
you gestated through the summer. A tomb
so hot it drove you mad. Your role was cast
before you were born. She felt by your kicks,
> deliberate, hard, that you would come out wrong.
> As the leaves were dying in September,
> you became yet another mouth to feed.
> Though the youngest, you were meant to belong
> in the middle. The onerous member,
> sprouted, cultivated from the bad seed.
You started drinking at eight. Ill-fated
sips of Grandpa's best whiskey, which he taught
you to swallow without wincing. He'd cheer,
belly laugh while you intoxicated
him with your little boy pratfalls. You bought
your first joint at nine. Made a quick career
> out of skipping school to sell your escape
> on the street. Carried a knife in your boot.
> She couldn't afford to notice. She lost
> what she wanted as her life to the rape
> of motherhood. With you the point was moot.
> Children that followed were simply the cost
of getting married, as herself a child,
in the nineteen-fifties. The drug of choice
was LSD. You supplied half the town
until our brother OD'd from a wild
excursion with you. Your once pleasant voice
turned raw from the fire of free-base. The down
> and up of your moods extreme. Tried to kill
> your lover after a binge. Beat your son
> and a twelve-year-old girl. Poor boy gone bad.
> Drown in self-pity. Says she loves you still,
> but washes her hands. Every brood has one
> she justifies. Wishes she never had.

You'll outlive them all, searching for a way
to elude reality by using
every means to fill some undefined need.
She'll die young. Relatively. Amusing,
don't you think, how her dreams turned to decay
from the life that grew out of one bad seed.

ON MY KNEES

a rime royale

Your poisoned finger's grip upon my heart
reduced the flow of blood into my brain.
An acrid aftertaste with lips apart,
a keepsake of your kiss. I touch the stain
between my legs, against my thigh. The rain
outside did mix with tears that drown the night,
that stung my eyes and took away my sight.

Beneath the mental image of your smile
you hid a sneer that held your true intent.
I heard your clever words, but all the while
was able to decipher what you meant.
The syllables, like shovels, made a dent
beneath my feet to bring me down to size.
While on my knees you stripped off your disguise

and held your manhood out for me to taste.
A thing you've done so many times before.
I wondered how it was I came to waste
this life. Diminished, kneeling on the floor
I drank your offering. In wanting more
than you could give, I cried unsatisfied
and begged for lips to smother mine. You lied

you loved me in the moment that you peaked,
and deep inside that moment I believed,
though in your wake remained a smell that reeked
of rotted passion, lust decayed. Deceived
by needs that turned grotesque, deformed, I grieved,
for you were all I'd hoped to have. I knew
an emptiness would come in place of you.

My body so familiar with the ground,
I'd rest my head beside my feet and wait
for you, and didn't care if I were found
exactly where you left me, with the hate
I carried for myself, curled with the fate
of seeing you again inside the fold
of legs and waist. The flooring tile was cold

against my face. I felt my heart constrict
with every thought of you, yet was compelled
to wait for what would never be, and tricked
myself with my own hand. My hunger quelled,
  self-gratified, until the tears that welled
up in my eyes had spilled and scarred my skin.
That's when you came and took from me again.

WETLANDS

Beneath the scraggy spurts of green,
between the stalks of brown and black,
lies a plate of tainted glass,
murky and fragmented
by tiny eruptions of moss.

Ripples flow as buoys glide
from one place to the next,
propelled by motors, webbed and invisible.
Miniature replicas follow close behind.
They form a line as if tied to a string.

Gossip resounds in chirps and croaks,
buzzes and whistles, twitters and hisses.
Acceptable apathy abounds, as one
is gobbled up by another,
they simply go about their business.

Along the periphery towering guardians
nod and wave with approval,
while civilizations inhabit
their heads, arms and torsos,
their feet buried deep within the ground.

As if superglued to their existence,
or bound by double-sided tape,
residents occasionally covet the winged
visitors, who fly in to holiday
in their summer cabins at the shore.

All day and night a chorus sings
in perfect half-billion part harmony.
The sky spirit Ariel circles above,
keeping rhythm and taking notes
which he will pass along to Gaea at a later date.

DEATH STANDS WAITING

a rondeau

Death stands waiting amidst the broken glass,
stains of booze on the walls, a smell of gas
from the kitchen. The air is thick with mold
and piss. Broken windows let in the cold
dead winter. Street sirens screech in, then pass.

Her head forced backward, mouth open. Your crass
tongue spitting venom down her throat. The mass
of words alone could kill, but you keep hold.
Death stands waiting.

You snap her neck, then proceed to harass
in a drunken rage no one can surpass.
Your breath reeks of cigarette smoke and old
vomit. You cry for sins you now amass.
Death stands waiting.

NOTHING BEAUTIFUL

inverted glose

The grotesque of me hidden inside bones,
at one time proudly danced across my face,
and children laughed and pointed at the child
they called a freak. Mothers' pitying stares

bore scars into my flesh, like cigarette
burns in a rug. I learned to emulate
the lovely, distorted the genetic
misfortunes that now survive on marrow.

A deal was struck, and so they are endless,
living subdermal, concealed by posture
and a smile to those who see from outside.
But I can only see me from within.

The ugly run along infrastructure,
travel with pulse through tissue and organ.
Seen solely by me in my reflection,
I always know what lies beneath my skin.

The grotesque of me hidden inside bones,
misfortunes that now survive on marrow,
living subdermal, concealed by posture.
Seen solely by me in my reflection.

IF I WERE A MAN

acrostic

Is it logical to assume that I would be
Fondling myself at all times of the day, not just

In private, but sometimes in public, avoiding

Watchful eyes of passersby, covering up my
Erection with the newspaper I've come to have
Ready for just such an occasion? Would I be
Ephebic in my demeanor, exploring myself

Adolescent-like, rummaging through the thick, coarse

Mounds of tightly woven hair around my penis?
As a woman I don't spend my days squeezing my
Nipples. But, I can see why you'd think that I would.

PRETTY GIRLS

Men don't like pretty girls who smoke
or swears that fall from a pretty girl's tongue.
Parents don't like it when pretty girls joke
about politics, sex or the plight of the young.
Teachers don't like it when pretty girls won't
let them favor them, touch them a time or two.
I know what not, and what pretty girls don't.
But I still don't know what ugly girls do.

Brothers hurt pretty sisters who steal Mother's love.
Fathers hurt pretty daughters who look like their wives
who are pretty no more, but are memories of
a time when they all lived prettier lives.
Girls resent pretty girls who tease and taunt
with thighs that are pretty and breasts that are too.
I know what they loathe and what pretty girls want.
But I still don't know what ugly girls do.

Young boys are afraid of a kiss or a touch
from a pretty young girl whose lips and caresses
remind him of his mother's too much.
Some pretty young boys don pretty pink dresses.
They're pretty young girls in the way they behave,
wearing a gender that's pretty and true.
I know what they fear and what pretty boys crave.
But I still don't know what ugly girls do.

Pretty girls laugh in ugly girl faces.
They point out your flaws and your ugly girl traits.
They cut you to size so you know where you place is.
A pretty girl tells you you're all that she hates
and would surely carry out the feat
of killing herself if she looked like you.
I know who they are, and how pretty girls cheat.
But I still don't know what ugly girls do.

DARK ENGLISH AFTERNOON
a rondeau

Dark English Afternoon tea builds sweat on my lip.
A splash of milk forms swirls of light. I take a sip.
Cream cheese sandwich, soup and a biscuit. I adore
the respite it brings from a hectic morning. More
than just a ritual. *The tea's the thing*, I quip.

Obscured sunlight through the gray, perfect for a trip
along the countryside. A few things to equip
my comfort, umbrella, sweater. But first I pour
Dark English Afternoon

to journey past the endless rapeseed fields. I rip
away fatigue with every taste. Both hands grip
the cup to feel the warm travel through each palm for
the wind can rattle straight through bone along the shore.
A shadow of France beneath Dover's white cliffs strip
dark English afternoon.

MOLIÉRE

a triolet

Moliére, the author of the Miser.
Harpagon kept his gold sealed in a tin.
You played the part, but were somewhat wiser.
Moliére, the author of the Miser,
you admired and became the deviser.
Found many effusive qualities in
Moliére, the author of the Miser.
Harpagon kept his gold sealed in a tin,

but you shared your wealth with all who wanted,
and understood the character so well.
We laughed as he hunched with chattels flaunted.
But you shared your wealth with all who wanted,
so in the end left the stage undaunted.
All around you applause began to swell,
but you shared your wealth with all who wanted,
and understood the character so well.

ABSENT OF HEART

Divine
right against the curve of rib,
the meeting place between breasts.
There is no tender embrace,
no sweet words spoken. Just space,
where hollow replaces heart
and echo replaces beat.
Silhouette, remembering

Divine
intervention of foreign
matter can't bring together
the one now broken apart,
ripped open, crushed or buried.
Hard to find all the pieces
that once made up the whole,
impossible if not for

Divine
providence accomplishes
nothing when the subject lies
prostrate in a field and waits
for hyenas and other
scavengers to pick the bone
and feast on flesh. Surrender
salvation, never to know

Divine
kingdom crumbles, spirit fades
with each calculated sin.
Vultures circle patiently.
Wait their turn to prey upon
what remains against the curve
of rib, inside the meeting
place between breasts, at one time

Divine.

JOURNEY TO A BETTER PLACE

a kyrielle

Tile hard against my heel. It jolts
the knee, an elastic that revolts
against the tightest stretch. Just four
more steps across the kitchen floor,

then I'll be there, away from here,
a softer place that holds a clear
view of something else. I explore
more steps across the kitchen floor

but elastic close to breaking,
snapping hard on my skin, making
scars. There isn't any detour.
More steps across the kitchen floor

the only way. Oh God, ahead
so far away. I fear, instead
that I may die right here. But for
more steps across the kitchen floor

I'd be dead. Just one. That's all. One
at a time. And soon I'll be done.
I don't know what there is in store.
More steps across the kitchen floor.

I'm standing in a softer space.
I know it is the very place
I longed to be four steps before.
More steps across the kitchen floor

to get back where I was. How could
I reason this other spot would
be better. It's dark. It hurts. Once more
more steps across the kitchen floor.

BLEEDING
a sestina

The odor is familiar, pungent, sweet.
It circles all senses just out of reach.
Caramelized sugar engulfed in decay,
tepid, hanging motionless in the air,
grows more acrid with each intake of breath.
Repugnant, concurrently compelling.
    Tile floor tacky under foot, compelling
    me to stay in this place, at one time sweet
    with innocence, now sour to my breath.
    Each step more cumbrous, attempting to reach
    the door to open and let in some air
    to help push out the lingering decay.
Unknown still is the source of the decay.
To discover it is more compelling
than any endeavor to clear the air.
Its revelation has become as sweet
as every ambition I've tried to reach.
I search, ignoring the burden of breath.
    I see no hint of stain. Discern no breath
    of scandal. Ahead, no sign of decay
    lends clues to the crime. Unable to reach
    a conclusion. Nagging, yet compelling,
    move forward, inching, while behind, the sweet
    stench grows stronger, permeating the air.
As if to thwart my goal, the sentient air
creeps up the line of my neck, chokes the breath
from weighted lungs. They fill instead with sweet,
vile elixir. I feel logic decay.
Although the drunkenness is compelling
I strain to keep my mission within reach.
    A final, labored step toward the door. Reach
    for the knob, open the portal. The air
    strikes my face, stings my lips, while compelling
    me to step outside and take in a breath
    unburdened. I turn to face the decay
    that trails at my feet. Surrender a sweet
sigh. Reach for the dripping blood. Snatch a breath
from the air with the knowledge the decay
comes from my wounds. Compelling. Bittersweet.

THE LOST DREAM

a rimas dissolutas

The slats on the Venetian blinds
were cracked just enough
for the light to slither through
and lay across my eyes.

The play inside my head unwinds.
Edges on the figures rough.
Then each character on cue
recited their goodbyes.

With stabbing knives the morning blinds.
My pupils pricked just enough
for blood to trickle through,
fall as tears from my eyes.

The players fade. The dream unwinds.
Sheets around my skin are rough.
Alarms ring in my head on cue
drowning out their last good-byes.

INSOMNIA

an envelope sonnet

A spark of light was caught under my lid.
It danced around the players in my mind.
Eyes closed against the night I saw it bind
with wire, the hands of slumber. It forbid

the characters from exiting the stage,
and brushed away the fuzzy start of sleep.
Without remorse, the miscreant would creep
while flashing faces in a disco rage.

To obviate the presence of repose
it traveled to the inside of my ear,
and drummed a beat that lingered to the day,
then laid a tickle deep inside my nose.
Made an announcement to all who could hear
to come audition for tomorrow's play.

OUTBURSTS

Dull little girl. Thin legs. Small breasts.
Look up to the shadow of fate.
Subdued by a touch. Requests
thrown in your face, like mud. His hate

spat from lips in careful hushed tone.
Wipe the residue from your skin
when he's not looking. When alone
cough up the self-loathing. The sin

of being born. Hide it below
newspaper, coffee grounds. Carry
it out to the trash right away so
he won't see your outburst. Very

clever, for a dull little girl.
Except for remnants left behind
you fool yourself for a while. Curl
up in a ball, sure he won't find

the stain under the rug made by
an overflowing bag of flaws
and insecurities, and lie
face down in bed, for the cause

of your pain escapes from your eyes
and murmurs deep within your sleep.
They're bothersome those muffled cries.
Annoys him. He says he cares deep

down. Then the side-glance, jagged word
meant to shut you up. Funny how
once it effectively deterred
you from potential outbursts. Now

you prattle with mindless chatter
and choose to flail and bleed
openly. What used to matter
you've abandoned. A fleeting need

to prove yourself. This petty tiff
will bring the hand of fate to hurl
you into place. You'd be cute if
you weren't such a dull little girl.

WITNESS TO A CLOUD ON A WINTER MOONLIT NIGHT

Cirrus drawn by full moon light,
and I, lured, like the tide, looked
to the heavens. A trail hooked
a perfect arch, left to right.

Single, thin, transparent line
bent along the lunar curve.
Without twist or sudden swerve.
Simple, as if to define

an eternal sky. Almost
mathematical. Abated
by the black beyond. Fated
by gravity of its host,

the earth, to completely loop
the world below. How strange,
that one cloud should rearrange
my concept of life. To scoop

the dominance from my brain,
for something Great must have made
this vapor, destined to fade
long before the moon should wane.

Crystal band across the orb,
illuminated clearly from within,
a center brightest, but thin
edged, where the dark did absorb

the endless translucent strip.
Its scope so wide with wonder.
I stood motionless under
the universe and took a sip.

A most transitory grace
which no mortal could create,
nor in image duplicate.
One again I'd never face.

But was blessed just once to see.
So lies my significance
in witnessing this brilliance.
Always in my memory.

IN THE KNOWING

Modest house, incessantly gray.
Shade trees that can't quite sprout for spring.
Crab grass jutting through clumps of clay,
turns to mud when the clouds sing.
>   Crooked front walk, cracked concrete block
>   connect the driveway to the stoop,
>   two steps, no rail. Closed-in porch, mock
>   elegance from the street and dupe
strangers who peer while roaming past.
View only pretty window lace,
eyelets misinterpret light cast
from a stand-up lamp. Shadowed grace
>   seen only by those who don't know
>   the close-up of you. The clutter,
>   shoes, boxes, papers strewn below
>   the line of sight. Trick and shutter
the world with distance and fences.
Never invite anyone in.
Days spent creating pretenses
instead of a home. Tales you spin
>   take more time than painting a wall.
>   My nose pressed against the screen. There
>   inside, uncomplicated, small
>   dingy rooms, pallid rugs and square
characterless cupboards above
messy kitchen counters. Easy
chair, lazy boy, on which you love,
I imagine, to watch cheesy
>   sci-fi TV shows, sits angled
>   indiscriminately among
>   videotapes, books and tangled
>   wires. Numerous magazines are flung
on a pressed wood coffee table.
How sad, you've kept me from knowing
you, and so was never able
to enjoy what you were showing

me. Tidy perfection, without
blemish. A life I could not touch,
but dreamt I wrapped my arms about.
In your jumble, I love you much
more. Now that I've stolen a peak
I see what others don't, my friend.
Of what I know I will not speak,
but will hold dear until the end.

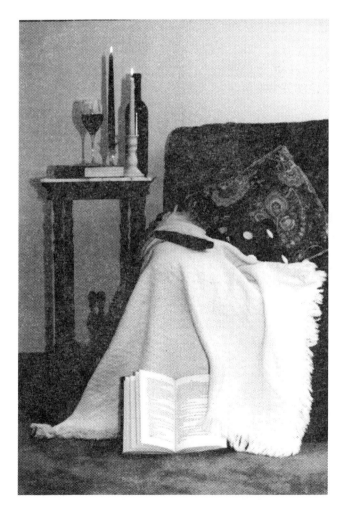

THE VISIT
triplets

If Death should visit while I sleep,
kneel beside the bed, inhale deep
breaths of life that quietly creep

from dreaming, would I know? Would fear
invade slumber? The end appear
as a mighty horned beast, draw near,

snatch my soul? Or, as it hovers,
smile in the meeting of lovers?
Would I fold back the bed covers,

invite Death to lie next to me,
embrace the dying, silently
surrender self eternally?

If Death should visit while awake,
walk through the kitchen door, sit, take
a moment to sip tea, read Blake

by morning light, would I listen?
Watch the immortal words glisten
before sun-drenched lace, then christen

this young forehead with a kiss? Or
would Death hide in the cellar, more
patient than pillar, prepared for

my descent, cunning, shadowed thief,
to steal my essence, prove belief
as truth or waste of time, while grief

settles along the baseboards, dust
on bookshelves, pictures, lamps and just
above the doorframe? Would I trust

the one hand outstretched, naked bone,
the other about a scythe, stone
cold finger pointing to the lone

passage leading into nether?
Should I go when Death comes, whether
it's bound by God or a tether

to below, or nothingness. Would
Death arrive uncovered, or hood
its face and trick me so I could

not see, follow blind through the gate
of unknown everything?   What fate
would be mine? I can only wait.

NIGHTMARE INFINITE
an English sonnet

I dreamed that right before I died, was ripped
apart by monster's teeth, whose feast began
about my toes, with careful nibbles, stripped
the flesh, exposed the underneath and ran
its tongue across the meat before it chewed
a tender piece from off the bone. I felt
no pain, but lay in awe as I reviewed
hyena wait and vulture perch. It knelt
before the meal of me with careful eye
upon the lazy ones who scavenge death.
The shapeless predator devoured each thigh,
then waist and gut and arms, then took a breath
and fell asleep and dreamed its underneath
was being torn apart by human teeth.

ANTIDEPRESSANTS

a triolet

One pill, take with milk, every night before I sleep.
A simple prescription to hammer out the black
that comes before the sorrow, independent, deep.
One pill, take with milk, every night before I sleep.
Collect the mind-invading, scattered pictures, heap
them together behind unstructured thoughts in back.
One pill, take with milk, every night before I sleep.
A simple prescription to hammer out the black.

Just a few side effects. I do as I am told.
Last resort to lift the chronic weight from my chest.
I wake up every morning slightly numb, and cold.
Just a few side effects. I do as I am told,
eager to swallow the synthetics I've been sold.
Ignore loss of self and sex, loss of words and rest.
Just a few side effects. I do as I am told.
Last resort to lift the chronic weight from my chest.

Colors denude from day. Dreams disappear from night.
Replace despondency with vacancy. Forget
vacancy with the onset of tremors. Dim, light
colors denude from day. Dreams disappear from night.
Dull, dispassionate existence, now mine, despite
the constant love from you. I don't know how I let
colors denude from day, dreams disappear from night.
Replace despondency with vacancy. Forget.

I used to write with ease. Now I don't write at all,
and cry because there's nothing left for me to do,
for it was in my darkest moments, I recall,
I used to write with ease. Now I don't write at all.
Purpose poured on the page, gave purpose to, though small
and fleeting, my depression. It was all I knew.
I used to write with ease. Now I don't write at all,
and cry, because there's nothing left for me to do.

TOO LATE

a rondel

Asleep, nude, but for the light from the hall
gently brushing your cheeks and eyes. It lays
another dimension on your dream, and plays
shadow games on the sheets. I heard you call

me to bed, my love, the way you do all
the time. I take you for granted these days.
Asleep, nude, but for the light from the hall
gently brushing your cheeks and eyes. It lays

a twisted image of me on the wall
above your head as I hover and gaze
at the perfect you, who, despite me, stays.
I slip my body next to yours and fall
asleep, nude, but for the light from the hall.

THE TRUTH OF HUMOR
an English Sonnet

The tiny lines around your eyes appear
whenever you begin to laugh because
you know the truth of humor and it's clear,
you know the rules of every game and laws
of every rule. A secret told to me
that you perchance should overhear, becomes
a challenge and the utmost mystery
to solve before you can move on, and numbs
your senses to the point of nothingness.
But somehow you pursue until the end
and know the truth without the need to guess.
The smile of knowing comes again, my friend,
upon your face, and one more line appears.
You grow another inch amongst your peers.

HAIKU

Cattails are on fire.
They generate no heat, yet
inflame sun's desire.

HAIKU STRING

1

At least two-hundred
birds, small, black, leaf the branches
of the baron oak.

2

Thatched homes of crumbled
tan and red, cement themselves
to ancient shoulders.

3

Rains lift the black road,
carry it elegantly
to puddle and sit.

4

Sun, though on the clock,
takes a noontime nap and lets
cloud work overtime.

5

February day ·
you let me see right through you
and what lives inside.

6

Brown, gray, yellow, you
hold these colors brilliantly
until the spring comes.

7

Spring swallows winter.
The bitch is so flamboyant
flowering the truth.

COAXING SLEEP

Sheets, crumpled at the foot of the bed
remain where I kicked them hours ago.
They are rough this night against my legs.
Despite the cold, I lie bare.

Concentrate on the ceiling instead
of the scamp that walks from chin to toe
and prickles and pokes and nags and begs
attention. Motionless, stare

at space directly above my head
between what is real and what I know.
Drudge up the sediment, ask the dregs
to overpower despair.

Ever motionless, it seems I've led
the devil away for a while, and so
a numb licks my skin and dreams and eggs
away all life from the air.

A TRUE STORY
a villanelle

I saw an imp scamper across the road.
Looked much like the skeleton of a bird
caught between headlights, blacktop and the rain.

Quick-footed and translucent, thought to bode
mischievous days ahead, a sight absurd.
I saw an imp scamper across the road,

bone-thin, backward knees. An arcane
creature, never meant to be seen or heard,
caught between headlights, blacktop and the rain.

Roams through the night and lives among the toad.
For a moment, its cloak of dark obscured.
I saw an imp scamper across the road.

The sight of it did instantly ordain
a new belief, one indistinct, and blurred,
caught between headlights, blacktop and the rain.

No higher than my calf and slightly bowed.
My sense of self-importance since deferred.
I saw an imp scamper across the road,
caught between headlights, blacktop and the rain.

AN ACCIDENTAL MEETING

a terza rima

Soprano chatter pranced between two girls,
a picket fence and tire swing, while mint
arose with playful grace from perfect curls.

Their song was carried through the dark and glint
of time and endless space and ageless age.
Romantic lyric laughing with a hint

of dirt just turned to sow. A wistful sage
pervaded every sleeping pore. Became
familiar without prior sense. A gage

that sparked a hesitance. Two girls who came
to always be two girls. To never grow
beyond their childhood fancy. Ever same.

But they were children I would never know.
Their incoherent musings passed this bed,
meandered by a shallow dream. Although

unable to interpret what was said,
it sang a distant choir, a melody
that slipped into and danced inside my head.

The most naïvely perfect reverie
escaped the dead and rambled to my ear.
Repose dissolved quite accidentally.

The chatter louder, more distinct, fell near.
A vacant room engulfed in voice, not mine,
and scent, not mine, had slapped my face, brought clear

abrupt awakening. It broke the line
dividing seemingly quiescent sound,
cavorting off the tongues of sprites divine,

and absolute reality. Profound
awareness in an instant. When I knew
I was alone, I heard the phrase resound

aloud. I sat up straight. As if on cue
the empty room at once alive with word,
not meant for me to hear, however true.

A frightening encounter for I'd heard
the banter of two girls whose death had come
too young. So, consciousness had not deterred

the final warning as if spoken from
the grave. *Be quiet she can hear us.* Still.
I saw no shadow, felt no chill, no hum,

no mint, no sage remained. The window sill
was thick with paint that sealed it shut. The door
was locked. I stayed awake against my will

and waited for the words I'd heard before.
Perhaps some movement, rustle, flash of light,
a little smoke outlining figures, or

another whisper, chirp, reflection might
reveal two girls, much like the photograph
discovered in the attic late one night,

eroded, faded, nearly torn in half
with time. Two girls aside a picket fence.
Not more than ten-years-old, each wore a laugh

eternal. Yes. I heard their innocence.
I smelled the mint that washed their hair.
They lived and died before my life, and hence

by happenstance, they found a sleep to share
a song. And I, the momentary host,
held sweetest music, smelled the fragrant air.

But found it faded quickly with the ghost.
So now, the only thing I know for sure,
the single phrase one spoke when I was most

awake. *Be quiet she can hear us.* Pure
expression of a child who died a score
before my birth. I pine for them, endure,

and wait and sleep and waste the day but for
the chance to hear and dream with them once more.

JUST BECAUSE...

A man I knew was murdered today.
Shot, point blank, in the back of the head.
Why he was killed is sketchy and gray,
but someone thought him better off dead.
Neither colleague, nor family, nor friend.
A man I knew.
        No one in the end.

ANTICIPATING RAIN

a rondelet

Supposed to rain.
Sad, overcast prediction.
Supposed to rain.
Drum the window, cloud my brain.
Stubborn sun, contradiction.
Downpours drench my addiction.
Supposed to rain.

ANTICIPATING DEATH

a rondelet

I'm not frightened
of Death, what lies in waiting.
I'm not frightened
of dying young. Enlightened
without faith. No debating
god, truth or life creating.
I'm not frightened.

WAITING

Wretched year. Despite the rain, despite
forbidding frost, bitter wind, while all
the sky is gray with cloud, all of night
shielding endless stars from earthly sight,
donning shirt sleeves I await the call

of spring. Nesting ducks hold the season
in their coats, unfettered, swim about
the murky water without reason
to the weather. An act of treason
in my blood as winter casts a doubt

upon the day. Legs a bit apart,
I stand with ankles bare, canvas shoes
soaked with icy dew, a torpid heart
anticipating warmth. A new start.
Past the equinox, you, winter, choose

to make your bed in this tainted soul.
Hold my one offense in frozen grip.
Befriend my one mistake that you stole
from what I barely recollect, roll
it over in review, then strip

every perfect, pleasant part of past.
Treasure true the one keepsake that broke
the want of he I could have loved. Last
year you knew, darling winter, how vast
expansive ice, crushing snow, would choke

any prudence left and plant a need
that grows a hollow heart. The baron land
was a clever tool you used to feed
a lust that pushed too hard, said too much. Greed
took from him until he could not stand

me. So here I stay, refuse defeat.
Killing chill finds refuge under skin,
paled by ebbing flow and slowing beat.
Living off the memory of heat.
Wait for spring to melt away my sin.

THE PAIN OF NOTHING

a rimas dissolutas

A
slow start.
Memory.
I let it walk
on paths of my brain
until it hits the end
and begins to pound its way
through the dark gray matter of wall.

I
take part
breaking me.
Begin to talk
to myself. Insane,
I know. Without a friend
it's hard to handle the day,
and so to keep from feeling small,

I
beat. Heart
a frenzy.
Strike harder. Block
memories. New pain
grows with each blow. Attend
the new that keep old at bay.
Less painful than nothing at all.

BIRTHRIGHT

There will never be any more of me.
The last was born in 1963.

But she of then became from circumstance,
so she of now, abandoning the dance

will never make another me of me.
The last was born in 1963.

She was aware of them and why she was.
By accident she carried on the cause.

A burden was the final me of me.
The last was born in 1963.

A reproductive chance that came up black.
Misfortune that could not be given back.

There can not be another me of me.
The last was born in 1963.

A GREATER NEED
a kyrielle

My need is greater than the kiss
that skims these lips with hesitance,
plays chase upon my face and lifts
a foolish countenance.

Wiser than the words that tumble
recklessly about the bed. Chance
revels in the hands that fumble
a foolish circumstance.

More than fleeting. Hard, mistreating,
fallible, fickle, greedy dance,
tramples love and truth while cheating
with foolish circumstance.

Abrasive passion flirts with hate
while ration hurts the heart. Your lance
though pointed, can not penetrate
my foolish countenance.

When shallow lust and hallow trust
compete to take the final stance,
I choose the latter, bring to dust
this foolish circumstance.

NEVER TRUST A CAT

She was licking his head.
Rough-tongued cleansing that lapped
a trustful condition.
He succumbed, but instead,
she raised her paw and slapped
him into submission.

DREAMING

In dream a broken window
sliver silver black and white
fragmented picture teased with dark
and muted light held captive. Spark
a sparkled scattered starlit night.
Cast queer reflection far below

the moon. Your love lies in shards of
fuzzy shadows on the floor. For
a single simple sliver you
love me. In dream. Fragmented, few
reflect a waking want. Explore
the mirrored dreaming of your love.

OPINION

an envelope sonnet

The music of the accolades turned sour.
The brass on the awards have tarnished since
you said you thought my poem lacked in power,
then yawned. As I explained, I saw you wince.
It's funny how the meter and the rhyme
and concrete images I've worked to link
have no effect on you, provoke no climb
of heartbeat or adrenaline. I think
you think abuse or anguish or neglect
are all the subjects I should write about.
No suicidal words, one might expect
I'd wasted every effort I'd put out.
You have, despite laudation from above,
diminished, with a phrase, the piece I love.

AUGUST

Too hot for dream, too wet for sheet.
Arrogant, haughty season queen.
I feel I could love you when you
are half the world away. But here,
on top of me, heavy, I fear
I will crush under your weight. Sweet
teasing air seduces the screen
while still cool, at a distance. Few

moments of perfect beguilement
before you wave over my skin,
crawl into my blood, then blackmail
my flesh, force me to bare belly,
back, legs and arms. Turn thick, smelly,
rancid, sticky when temperament
quickens and the night becomes thin.
Your once resplendent light grows pale

as days grow too long to endure.
How easily you sweep through sleep,
nestle comfy into each curve,
dupe me into craving your warm
embrace. Meanwhile, beyond, the swarm
of night breaks its seemingly pure
black stillness, as it starts to creep,
buzz, drone and jangle every nerve.

You loved me when I was a child.
You played with me like an older
sister. Beckoned me outside where
thunderstorms and rainbows delight.
Where breezes, made for me, took flight.
I remember how your sun smiled
on water, whose first touch colder
than Winter, held hands with the air.

But I grew, and you noticed me
noticing Spring. It comes with age,
appreciating the rebirth.
Jealous girl. You don't like to share.
Insecure, you think I compare
you with your siblings. Don't you see,
I loved you separately. Now rage
fills these days. My part of the earth

becomes your revenge because I
dared to grow up, want more than you.
Summer, I miss what was before.
Arrogant, haughty season queen.
Why do you have to be so mean?
Dusk shrouded with mosquito sky.
Window sheers drenched with evening dew
and you don't love me anymore.

THE DYING TIME

a pantoum

October, November. Dying months. Raw
chill, romanticized as nip in the air,
seeps through the cracks in the windows and doors,
while rot takes over the earth. Rain's shriving

chill, romanticized as nip in the air,
rips through the tree's overcoat, strips it bare,
while rot takes over the earth. Rain's shriving
laughter rattles the roof. Ravaging wind

rips through the tree's overcoat, strips it bare.
Brilliant pink and green turned brown. All is gray.
Laughter rattles the roof. Ravaging wind,
I envy your force on the world. To be

brilliant pink and green turned brown. All is gray.
Simple. Defined lines without camouflage.
I envy your force on the world. To be
scoured of the year. Absolved, new. Sweet autumn

seeps through the cracks in the windows and doors.
Simple defined lines without camouflage.
October, November. Dying months. Raw.
Scoured of the year. Absolved, new. Sweet Autumn.

EXPOSED
an English sonnet

I watched you as you peeled away my skin,
and felt the rush of air across each nerve.
You started slowly underneath my chin.
The angle made it awkward to observe.
Then with a sudden wrench betrayed my chest,
and blood spurt up into my mouth and eyes.
Through stinging tears I saw my blurry breast,
the tissue ripped. My heart heaved in surprise
from its abrupt encounter with the world,
unable to conceal its frantic beat.
The fluid in my veins raced forth and swirled
into my brain, then dropped into my feet.
You left me standing in my vertigo
exposing what I did not want to show.

IMAGINING HAIKU

1
Imagining Life…

within fragile walls
windows darkened by winter
spring knocks, waits, withers

2
Imagining Song…

fluting sunrise lifts
your gable above the cloud
oboe sings within

3
Imagining Green…

grass along your walk
where I stand, alone beyond
your front door, yellows

4
Imagining You…

knew me once before
the autumn night held your heart
leaving me outside

MANIPULATING HAIKU

Juggle me, but please
wait until it's cool enough
so I don't throw up

Eileen Albrizio

noted for writing in formal verse, was a member of the 1998
Connecticut national poetry slam team, and is a member of the
celebrated writer's circle *Artemis Rising*. An award-winning
playwrite and poet, Eileen's plays **What's a Mother For?** (co-
authored by Connie-Magnan Albrizio) and **Rain** have been rec-
ognized by the *Writer's Digest* as one of the best plays of 1996
and 1997 respectively. She studied undergraduate theatre at
Central Connecticut State University and graduate playwriting
at Weslyan Univeristy in Middletown, Connecticut. Eileen be-
gan a career in broadcast news in 1994, received the *1996 Con-
necticut Associated Press Best Newscast Award*, and currently
works for Connecticut Public Radio, a member station of Na-
tional Public Radio, as a news anchor and reporter. Eileen and
her husband, Wayne Horgan, own a comic book store in Rocky
Hill, Connecticut called Heroes & Hitters. The two live in the
Hartford area with their three cats, Trouble, Buddy and Smokee.